T0194083

Theological Positions on WORSHIP

Michael Amoah PhD

WESTBOW
PRESS®
A DIVISION OF THOMAS NELSON
& ZONDERVAN

WestBow Press books may be ordered through booksellers or by contacting:

WestBow Press
A Division of Thomas Nelson & Zondervan
1663 Liberty Drive
Bloomington, IN 47403
www.westbowpress.com
1 (866) 928-1240

ISBN: 978-1-9736-4120-9 (sc)
ISBN: 978-1-9736-4121-6 (hc)
ISBN: 978-1-9736-4119-3 (e)

Library of Congress Control Number: 2018911565

Print information available on the last page.

WestBow Press rev. date: 10/04/2018

Dedicated
to

The Minstrel Mary Ghansah

Contents

Contents

Preface

In the summer of 2010, while under a Palgrave Macmillan contract to author a book on a totally different subject (International Politics), the Holy Spirit interrupted that work for two weeks, because He wanted me to write this book on worship. Each time I attempted to continue with what I was working on, the Holy Spirit came upon me so strongly, and I was not at liberty to continue with that exercise. Instead I received liberty to write on worship. This continued throughout those two weeks, and the anointing did not lift until I had finished writing this manuscript on worship, now entitled "Theological Positions on Worship." The book which the Holy Spirit interrupted is now a popular academic book entitled "Nationalism, Globalization, and Africa," published by Palgrave Macmillan in November 2011.

Second, when it dawned on me what the Lord was doing – constraining me to write a book on worship, I attempted to familiarize myself with any existing material on the subject of worship, to see what has already been written, in order to decide what more I should like to say. The Lord instructed me not to copy from any existing material, but to write from what He had taught me directly on the subject of worship over the years. In other words, He wanted me to be very original to Him. I therefore began by referring to my own preaching tape that was recorded in London Kensington Temple on Saturday night 20 May 1995. I recall that I had briefly taught on some of the material on that tape at the Tema Community Two Salvation Army Corps in 1988. It also occurred to me, that over the course of 15 years since that 1995 tape recording, I had personally not heard similar teaching elsewhere since I had been in England. I immediately realized the importance of why God wanted me to be original, why He wanted me to write on worship, and precisely what He wanted me to convey. I appreciated His instructions and obeyed.

This book sets out the biblical, doctrinal, and theological positions on worship and praise. It has some technical content, for example it will tell you in the Introduction, and further explain in Chapters 1 and 3, that if you are not born-again, you cannot worship God the Creator of the Universe in spirit. Among other things, this book can teach and equip, so you can consider it as a teaching manual. It can also help any reader to prune off misconceptions about worship and keep the refined positions based on the word of God. The Bible says: "For the word of God is living and powerful, and sharper than any two-edged sword, piercing even to the division of soul and spirit, and of joints and marrow, and is a discerner of the thoughts and intents of the heart" (Hebrews 4:12). We know that the sociological and cultural background of a people can influence their ways and style of worship, but the Word of Whom we worship is the standard, and will cut through the culture. Hence this book is both theological and sociological, and addresses a predominantly Christian audience, even if the last chapter (Chapter 14) is for both Christians and non-Christians. This book can also serve as a textbook for Bible Schools, Theology Seminaries and Religious Studies departments of academic institutions, and of course the praise and worship department of any Christian church.

The book covers a wide range of topics and issues including: the ministry of the minstrel; the biblical doctrine on both individual and congregational worship; the biblical and established order of worship in the church; the role of worship in warfare; the role of music in worship; prophetic praise; dancing in church; dressing and culture; the role of worship in deliverance; giving as an act of worship; and God's plan of restoration to worship.

Each chapter in the book begins with a list of the key texts or biblical references that feature in the chapter. In the course of the chapter, the appropriate reference appears in brackets alongside the issue being discussed, for example: The Bible instructs us to praise and worship with music (Psalm 149:3), just to help the reader know where and how the theological position has assumed or has been formulated. All scripture quotations in this book are from the New King James Version (Thomas Nelson).

God bless you as you read.

August 2018

Introduction

Key Texts

- ✓ Psalm 149:3
- ✓ Hebrews 12:22–24
- ✓ Psalm 148
- ✓ John 1:12–13 ; John 4:23–24

Introductory Points

Worship is not singing, is not a slow song, and may not be quiet, although all these can be part of worshiping.

Praise is not a fast song, is not always musical, and may not even be noisy, although fast pace, music and noise can be part of praising. However, the Bible instructs us to praise and worship with music (Psalm 149:3) even if you are also able to praise and worship without music. Music is a medium that God created to make praising and worshiping easier because it lubricates your mind and releases your emotions.

A praise song does not have to be fast, and a worship song does not have to be slow.

The lyrics of a song determine whether it is a praise song or a worship song. If the lyrics are praising God, then the song is a praise song regardless of a slow pace and whether or not it includes instrumentation or noise. Likewise, if the lyrics are worshiping God, then the song is a worship song regardless of a fast pace, cacophony or noise. It matters significantly whether the individual singing is born-again or not (John 1:12–13), because all living beings as well as God's creation including the trees, clouds, sun, moon, stars have the ability to praise God (Psalm 148:1–13), but only the saints (those who are saved or born-again) can worship, or engage God in worship, spirit-to-Spirit (John 4:23–24).

Hebrews 12:22–24 states: "But you have come to Mount Zion, to the heavenly Jerusalem, the city of the living God. You have come to thousands upon thousands of angels in joyful assembly, to the church of the firstborn, whose names are written in heaven. You have come to God, the judge of all men, to the spirits of righteous men made perfect, to Jesus the mediator of a new covenant, and to the sprinkled blood that speaks a better word than the blood of Abel."

The above quotation from the book of Hebrews makes a distinction between all men (the whole of humanity) and the spirits of righteous men made perfect (only those who are born-again). Zion in scripture always signifies the body of Christ or the church, even though not all who attend church services are born-again, and a congregation can consist of both the saved and unsaved. The scripture in Hebrews 12:22–24 give us an understanding, that when a congregation of any size are involved in praise and worship, that corporate activity unites with an assembly of angels. During that corporate activity, God passes judgement on each individual's praise because all men can praise God, however only those who are of the new covenant, born-again or saved, or whose names are written in heaven, will be worshiping, simply because God is a Spirit and only a born-again spirit can worship Him spirit-to-Spirit, or in spirit and in truth (John 4:24). Those already born-again are the true church, even though everyone in that particular meeting is also in church. In the process of that corporate activity or church service, if the unsaved ones are convicted by the Holy Spirit, and are willing, they may come to salvation, and join the church of the first born. Also, although God's creation, and all living things, can offer praise (Psalm 148:1–13), it is only the praise of the saints (those already saved or born-again) that God exalts (Psalm 148:14).

Chapter 1

Definitions of Worship

Key Texts

- ✓ Job 38:18 ; Job 37:5
- ✓ Psalm 148:1–13
- ✓ John 4:24
- ✓ 1 Chronicles 29:20 ; Daniel 2:46 ; Job 9:13
- ✓ Exodus 1:14 ; 1 Corinthians 9:13 ; Isaiah 14:3 ; Acts 7:7
- ✓ 1 Kings 1:16 ; Esther 3:5
- ✓ Romans 12:1
- ✓ Luke 7:45
- ✓ Psalm 89:7 ; Malachi 1:6 ; Hebrews 12:28
- ✓ 1 Samuel 2:30 ; Proverbs 14:31 ; Proverbs 3:9
- ✓ Acts 17:25
- ✓ 1 Chronicles 29:11–13 ; Matthew 6:9–10

Just as the ministry of the minstrel manifested in biblical times long before minstrelsy took form in England in medieval times, the original Hebrew and Greek words for the various demonstrations of worship in the Bible existed before the English language. Hence, the English word *worship*, as we know it, may not capture the full meaning of everything that worship entails. *Worship* as an English word is derived from the Old English *worthscipe*, meaning "worthiness." This means one offers to God because He is worth it.

Indeed, English is not the only language that finds itself inadequate to capture the originalities or vastness of worship, and even the original tongues of humanity prior to Arabic, Hebrew, Greek, and Aramaic cannot express the fullness of God. God is beyond comprehension; we can only try our best to describe or comprehend Him, yet He is forever incomprehensible. God says in Job 38:18, "Have you comprehended the breadth of the earth? Tell Me, if you know all this." And Job 37:5 says, "God thunders marvelously with His voice; He does great things which we cannot comprehend."

After the death and resurrection of Jesus Christ, worship is rendered by the spirit of a born-again Christian unto God. However, we must understand that although all living beings can offer sacrifices of thanksgiving and praise (Psalm 148:1–13), not all can worship (John 4:24). The outworking of worship, the fruit, or the physical manifestations of worship may take several forms in the relationship with God, including giving. There may be innumerable words that mean worship. The following are a just few examples of Hebrew and Greek words in the Bible that spring to my mind immediately. They illustrate or demonstrate worship in one form or another.

Hebrew

- *caged / segad / sawgad* – to prostrate (1 Chronicles 29:20 / Daniel 2:46 / Job 9:13)
- *abad / awbad* – to serve in bondage or execute a job (Exodus 1:14 / 1 Corinthians 9:13 / Isaiah 14:3 / Acts 7:7)
- *shachah / shawkaw* – to bow in homage or obeisance (1 Kings 1:16 / Esther 3:5)

Greek

- *latreuo* – a hired servant ministering; a reasonable service (Romans 12:1)
- *proskuneo* – kiss (Luke 7:45)
- *sebomai* – reverence or devotion (Psalm 89:7 / Malachi 1:6 / Hebrews 12:28)
- *sebazomai* – to honor religiously (1 Samuel 2:30 / Proverbs 14:31 / Proverbs 3:9)
- *therapeuo* – serve with your handiwork (Acts 17:25).
- *latreia* – adoration (1 Chronicles 29:11–13 / Matthew 6:9–10)

Chapter 2

The Biblical Pattern of Praise and Worship

Key Texts

- ✓ Psalm 100:4
- ✓ 2 Corinthians 9:10
- ✓ Leviticus 5:11
- ✓ Matthew 21:8–10
- ✓ Matthew 18:20
- ✓ John 4:23–24

Psalm 100:4 states, "Enter his gates with thanksgiving and into his courts with praise; give thanks to him and praise His name." This teaching or command, which tells worshipers the attitude with which one must proceed from the gate, also reveals the floor plan, outlay, or pattern of the temple and has become an order of service for the body of Christ or the church. This floor plan did not differ too much from the various temples that were built from time to time, such as Solomon's, Herod's, or the Jerusalem temple. The Jewish tabernacle (that was a precursor of the Jewish temple) was a miniature and portable temple and had a similar floor plan to the temple complexes that were built later. Indeed, the outlay of the tabernacle is the original plan from which the temples were subsequently constructed.

Obviously one enters the temple complex by the gate, which then leads into the courtyard (or courts). This is a very large area where people circulate, socialize, fraternize, and trade while obtaining or preparing their animals and other items for sacrifice. There were traders in the courtyard selling items for sacrifice. The scenario is a wide-open space that accommodated all manner of affairs and transactions. The sheer width of the space provided for public expression. This included dancing for those who

- were rejoicing because God had done something for them or provided them with a sacrifice to bring before Him (2 Corinthians 9:10);
- had found and purchased the right sacrifice, whether a turtledove, pigeon, lamb, or flour, since there were precise instructions on what sacrifice to bring as tailored for what purpose (Leviticus 5:11);
- wanted to dance for any reason.

The courtyard was a place for public expression. Symbolically, the courts of praise became the sites for demonstrating the outward expression of how one felt inside. Subsequently, the acts of praise could take place anywhere else as necessary. For example, when Jesus entered Jerusalem (e.g., the triumphal entry in Matthew 21:8–10), the multitude spread their clothes on the floor, while others cut down tree branches and spread on the floor for Him to walk on. The multitude also expressed their feelings vocally: "Hosanna to the Son of David! Blessed is He who comes in the name of the LORD! Hosanna in the highest!" (Matthew 21:9). However, the expressions of praise had no formula, was random, and occurred in whatever manner that the people felt to do. Please note that there is no formula. This is a central point to which we shall revisit in Chapter 7 of this book.

Without presenting all the detail from the temple's outlay, we know that from the courtyard, the temple complex progressed into the Holy Place and ended up in the Holy of Holies, where only the high priest entered annually on the Day of Atonement and where the Ark of the Covenant dwelled. In these holy sections of the temple, there was no praise or fanfare, only worship, and petitions made by the priests. We know that the altar of sacrifice was located in front of the porch (in Herod's temple) and at the main entrance (in Solomon's temple). The distinction that is useful to know is that praise took place in the courtyard and worship took place beyond the courtyard.

A corporate sequence along the biblical pattern has been occurring within the corporate body or congregation, which has become an order of service for the body of Christ or the church. After the death and resurrection of Jesus Christ, when each born-again believer can worship God individually and separately (John 4:24), this corporate sequence does not mean that individual members of a congregation are not already before the Lord or the throne of heaven (in the Holy Place or Holy of Holies, so to speak). The sequence is therefore merely an order of service for the corporate body or congregation of any size with a quorum of two persons (Matthew 18:20). The sequence or order of worship can sometimes be religious because it is not always necessary that the congregation should go through the motions of praise if it can be judged that the presence of the Holy Spirit is already mighty and at hand; therefore the "worship" can sometimes precede the "praise," and the worship leader has to discern the appropriate way to lead or what sequence the Holy Spirit wants for the meeting, corporate body, or quorum at the time. Similarly, if individuals are constantly walking in thanksgiving and in praise, as well as in tune or close fellowship with the Lord, they may simply proceed into God's throne room without going through the motions of the religious pattern, and they may not even have to be musical about it: the true worshipers shall worship in spirit and in truth (John 4:24).

Chapter 3
True Worshipers and Liberation from the Venue

Key Texts

- ✓ John 4:19–24
- ✓ Psalm 146:1–2; Psalm 148:1–14
- ✓ Mark 7:6–7 ; Isaiah 29:13
- ✓ Hebrews 12:22–24
- ✓ Hebrews 10:25
- ✓ Psalm 22:3
- ✓ Hebrews 13:5
- ✓ Matthew 18:20

The Samaritan woman said, "Our fathers worshiped on the mountain [a venue] and you Jews say Jerusalem is the place where one ought to worship [another venue]" (John 4:20). Jesus replied,

> Woman, believe Me, the hour is coming when you will neither on this mountain, nor in Jerusalem [venueless], worship the Father … But the hour is coming, and now is, when the true worshipers will worship the Father in spirit and truth; for the Father is seeking such

> to worship Him. God is Spirit, and those who
> worship Him must worship in spirit and truth
> (John 4:21, 23–24)

The scripture passage in John 4:19–24 gives us the two most important revelations about worship.

1. Only born-again spirits, or those born of God (John 1:12–13), can worship God, because God is a Spirit and true worshipers must worship Him in spirit and in truth (John 4:24), even though all of God's creation have the ability to praise God (Psalm 148:1–13) and all living beings can praise God (Psalm 146:1–2).

2. The venue where you are does not matter, whether on the mountain, in Jerusalem, at work, on the train, in games, or even in the washroom. You can always worship. The unsaved can praise God but cannot worship in spirit. Only the saved can both praise and worship in spirit. Furthermore, it is only the praise of the saved (or the saints) that God has exalted (Psalm 148:14). Unless you are born-again, you cannot worship God, the Creator of the universe.

Furthermore, God made clear the distinction between lip service and worship, when Jesus said to the Pharisees and scribes that it is vain to attempt worship not from the heart (Mark 7:6–7).

Also, Hebrews 12:22–24 states,

> But you have come to Mount Zion, to the
> heavenly Jerusalem, the city of the living God.
> You have come to thousands upon thousands of
> angels in joyful assembly, to the church of the
> firstborn, whose names are written in heaven.
> You have come to God, the judge of all men, to
> the spirits of righteous men made perfect, to
> Jesus the mediator of a new covenant, and to the
> sprinkled blood that speaks a better word than
> the blood of Abel.

Therefore, unless you are part of the new covenant that was negotiated or mediated by the shedding of the blood of Jesus Christ, you are not saved, you are not part of the church of the first born, and your name is not written in heaven.

The above discussion liberates us from any thinking that we have to be in the company of other believers before we can worship. However, this should not be an excuse to refrain from fellowshiping, or worshiping in the company of other believers, because the Bible encourages us not to forsake the assembling of ourselves together (Hebrews 10:25). Also, because God inhabits the praises of His people (Psalm 22:3), there are some visitations from God which you can only experience in the midst of a company of believers, or in a congregation. Because God inhabits the praises of His people, even though the Spirit of God dwells in each saved

11

person, and furthermore God says that He will never leave nor forsake you (Hebrews 13:5), there is an extra or corporate manifestation of the presence of God that can only occur and does occur each time a company of believers meet together or praise God together (Psalm 22:3 / Matthew 18:20); and that corporate presence is not something you want to be missing.

Chapter 4

Understanding Worship as the Highest Form of Warfare

Key Texts

- ✓ 1 Chronicles 16:6
- ✓ 2 Chronicles 20:14–17 ; 2 Chronicles 20:21–23
- ✓ Psalm 22:3
- ✓ Romans 8:31
- ✓ Joshua 6
- ✓ Acts 16:16–38
- ✓ Psalm 149:6–8
- ✓ Psalm 144:1–2

It occurred during the reign of King Jehoshaphat, that even though God had already spoken publicly through Jahaziel the prophet and trumpeter (2 Chronicles 20: 14–17 ; 1 Chronicles 16:6) that Judah was going to win the battle against the Moabites, Ammonites, and the inhabitants of Mount Seir, and had even revealed details of the enemy's battle plan to them (2 Chronicles 20:16), Jehoshaphat received some last minute intelligence from the Lord about how the army should proceed, and subsequently issued those specific instructions. One would have thought that these would be military instructions, but not. Instead, he appointed singers to the battle front and ordered them to minister before the Lord the **song of the time** along the following lyrics: "Praise the Lord, For His mercy endures forever" (2 Chronicles 20:21). The Bible states that "When they began to sing and to praise, the Lord set ambushes against the people of Ammon, Moab and Mount Seir who had come up against Judah; and they were defeated" (2 Chronicles 20:22), in accordance with the word of the Lord from Jahaziel the Levite that "... the battle is not yours but God's" (2 Chronicles 20:15). The Bible says that God inhabits the praises of his people (Psalm 22:3) and when this happens, God's presence in the situation becomes the weapon against the enemy. Your adversary, or the situation you are facing contrary to the purposes of God will then find themselves facing God, and if God is for you, who or what can be against you (Romans 8:31)?

In a similar experience during the battle of Jericho, even though God told Joshua: "See! I have given Jericho into your hand, its king, and the mighty men of valor" (Joshua 6:2), God gave last minute instructions which were not military at all, but simply: that seven Levitic trumpeters should proceed before the Ark of the Covenant that led the army, and blow their trumpets; the trumpeters should lead the march with trumpeting; and the rest of the army should respond to the sound of the trumpets with a great shout when Joshua gives the order; and march around the city with that strategy. On the seventh march of the seventh day, after this sequence of trumpeting in front of the army, the rest of the marchers shouted when Joshua gave the order, and the wall of Jericho came tumbling down (Joshua 6:3–21). Again, the Lord inhabited the praises of His people Israel (Psalm 22:3) and God's presence in the situation became the weapon against the enemy. When this happens, your adversary, or the situation you are facing contrary to the purposes of God will find themselves facing God, and if God is for us, who or what can be against us (Romans 8:31)?

A New Testament example of how God can butt into a situation when praise is present, occurred in Acts 16:16–38 when Paul and Silas were imprisoned because Paul had cast out a familiar spirit with which a fortune-teller operated, and the mafia or proprietors of the fortune-telling business engineered for Paul and Silas to be imprisoned. While they were in prison, the two were "praying and singing hymns to God" (Acts 16:25) and God inhabited the situation with an earthquake and broke the chains of all the prisoners. As a result, the jailer treated the wounds of Paul and Silas and released them from prison. Moreover, the jailer and his household accepted Jesus Christ and were baptized.

We must understand that it is for our own assistance that God has ordained praise as a form of warfare, simply because praise is what God inhabits (Psalm 22:3). Your praise is therefore a weapon against the enemy, or if you prefer, God becomes the weapon against your enemies when God inhabits your praises. Praise and warfare therefore go hand in hand. The psalmist caught this revelation and stated: "Let the high praises of God be in their mouth, and a two-edged sword in their hand, to execute vengeance on the nations, and punishments on the peoples; to bind their kings with chains, and their nobles with fetters of iron; to execute on them the written judgement – this honor have all His saints. Praise the Lord!" (Psalm 149:6–9). The psalmist also stated: "Blessed be the Lord my Rock, who trains my hands for war, and my fingers for battle – my loving kindness and my fortress, my high tower and my deliverer, my shield and the One in whom I take refuge, who subdues my people under me" (Psalm 144:1–2). It does not take rocket science to conclude that when you indulge in praise and worship, or allow yourself to be trained in praise and worship, you have trained yourself for war.

Chapter 5

The Ministry of Singing (Music)

Key Texts

- ✓ Psalm 100:2
- ✓ Psalm 149:3
- ✓ Psalms 33:3; 96:1; 98:1; 144:9; 149:1
- ✓ Isaiah 42:10 ; Romans 8:26
- ✓ Acts 16:16–38

Psalm 100:2 states: "come before His presence with singing." Also, Psalm 149:3 states: "Let them praise his name with dancing and make music to him with tambourine and harp."

Music is a medium of communication – a means of fellowshiping with the Holy Spirit. Music can penetrate the soul, and release emotional stress, hurts and hatred. Therefore music can help you detox emotionally and spiritually. It can also prepare the ground for the word of God to penetrate and divide assunder your soul and spirit (Hebrews 4:12), hence the established tradition of song ministration before the preaching. Music is an effective means of communication. It is also God's weapon of administering judgement against our enemies. Music is what the Lord can inhabit, and fight on our behalf (Psalm 22:3), as we have seen with Jehoshaphat, with Joshua at Jericho, and with Paul and Silas when they were in prison.

The Bible instructs us in several places to sing a new song unto the Lord (Psalm 33:3; 96:1; 98:1; 144:9; 149:1; Isaiah 42:10, etc.). The new song reflects where we are in our journey with God, and enables us to keep in step with Him. The new song expresses how we feel towards Him in real time or prophetically, and expresses what we say to Him at prophetic times of our lives. Singing the same song all the time is an indication that you are on the same page with God, as if God is not doing anything new, or not doing anything at all. Therefore when the Bible instructs us to sing a new song, the Holy Spirit is helping us to keep in step with God, or respond to God in a timely way or in real time, and be sensitive to Him.

Music and grief, distress, groaning

Sometimes when you are emotionally distressed, or in a difficult situation, you may be too distressed to pray, you may be at a loss for words, you simply may not know in what form to express how you feel, your expression or prayer may sound like a confused noise (cacophony), and your soul may find expression through singing, which may be your only lubricant in the mechanics of that difficult situation or distress. Indeed every sound (including noise) is music, and if you take time to carefully string along the individual sounds, a melody will emerge. We know that when you are distressed you may not have the time make out what the melody is, let alone care about the musical notes of that melody. When you do not know what to say, how to say it, or how to intercede, the groaning of your soul/spirit by the work of the Holy Spirit is the intercession with groanings which cannot be uttered (Romans 8:26). In other words, groaning is also music. When Paul and Silas were imprisoned, they were "praying and singing hymns to God" (Acts 16:25) when God dramatically intervened in the situation, and effected their release. We know for a fact that Paul and Silas were not singers or musicians, and we don't know what cacophony they made, all we know is that they prayed and sang, and their breakthrough came. So when God says we should come before His presence with singing (or music), He is only trying to help us communicate what our words alone may not be able to express. So, just express yourself anyhow and let God determine what music it is that you are communicating. As mentioned at the beginning of this chapter, music is a medium of communication.

Chapter 6

Prophetic Praise

Key Texts

- ✓ Luke 1
- ✓ Isaiah 9:2
- ✓ Luke 2:29–32
- ✓ Isaiah 55:11
- ✓ Exodus 15:20
- ✓ 2 Chronicles 20:21–23
- ✓ Joshua 6
- ✓ 2 Timothy 2:15
- ✓ Revelation 4:1–11
- ✓ Ephesians 5:19
- ✓ Colossians 3:16

Prophetic praise is determined by any or all of the following:

- When an utterance of praise forecasts or predicts event(s) to come;
- When the selection of song is expressly given by the Holy Spirit (ditto);
- When an act of praise (gestures, dance, or instrumentation) is prophetically inspired or manifested by divine direction.

When the utterance of praise forecasts or predicts

Whether in the euphoria of the moment, in response to an event, or at any given time, the utterance of an individual's praise becomes predictive of things to come, then the utterance can be regarded as obviously prophetic. The beginning chapters of the Gospel of Luke has good examples of prophetic praise. We find in this portion of scripture, that after Mary had received the word from Angel Gabriel that she was to become the mother of Jesus, and she had accepted this role (Luke 1:26–38), Elizabeth prophetically praised her cousin Mary the mother of Jesus in the following words:

- Blessed are you among women, and blessed is the fruit of your womb! But why is this granted to me, that the mother of my Lord should come to me? For indeed, as soon as the voice of your greeting sounded in my ears, the babe leaped in my womb for joy. Blessed is she who believed, for there will be a fulfilment of those things which were told her from the Lord (Luke 1:42–45).

In response to the above praise, Mary also entered into prophetic praise (to the Lord) and her utterance has become popularly known as the Magnificat (Luke 1:46–55). In the course of this praise, Mary prophesied "... For behold, henceforth all generations will call me blessed" (Luke 1:48).

After this incident, Elizabeth gave birth to her child whose father Zacharias was muted, and so was asked to name the child in writing. As soon as Zacharias had written down the child's name as John, he regained his speech and uttered prophetic praise in Luke 1:68–79. Within this long praise utterance from Zacharias, we find the following quote in accordance with the calling of John the Baptist who paved the way for the ministry of Jesus Christ, as well as to confirm what was in Isaiah 9:2, neither of which had been mentioned by Angel Gabriel:

- ... And you, child, will be called the prophet of the Highest; For you will go before the face of the Lord to prepare His ways ... To give light to those who sit in darkness and the shadow of death ... (Luke 1:76–79).

There was also a devout Jew known as Simeon, whose prophetic praise has become popularly know as the Nunc Dimittis. The Holy Spirit once revealed to him that he won't die until he had seen Jesus Christ. Therefore at the same time as Joseph and Mary took baby Jesus into the temple to dedicate him as the first male child according to tradition, Simeon was also led there by the Holy Spirit (Luke 2:21–27). Simeon then took Jesus into his arms and offered prophetic worship unto the Lord in the following words:

- Lord, now You are letting Your servant depart in peace, According to Your word; For my eyes have seen Your salvation which You have prepared before the face of all peoples, a light to bring revelation to the Gentiles, and the glory of Your people Israel (Luke 2:29–32).

When the song selection is expressly from the Holy Spirit

When a leader picks up a direction from the Holy Spirit that a particular song should be ministered, or when a person picks up the song as led by the Holy Spirit, or when the Holy Spirit dictates the selection of song to the leader, the result is prophetic praise. We can refer to that particular song as the **song of the time**, and if at all possible, the leader should not resist the Holy Spirit about the **song of the time**; indeed the song leader or worship leader should seek the Holy Spirit for such directions as to what the **song of the time** should be. Just as scripture states in Isaiah 55:11 that: "So shall My word be that goes forth from My mouth; it shall not return to Me void, But it shall accomplish what I please, and it shall prosper in the thing for which I sent it," so it is that God knows why the Holy Spirit is directing that particular **song of the time** to be ministered or used in worship. In Exodus 15:1–18, Miriam the minstrel who was in a mood with the Holy Spirit (or in tune with God) directed that a song be sang, and also dictated (or authored) the lyrics of the song.

So what about choir rehearsals and all the time and effort spent to rehearse prior to an event or performance? Are they a waste of time? No! Just as we ought to be familiar with the logos or written scriptures, we should treat the repertoire of songs that have been rehearsed as our "logos", and the **song of the time** which the Holy Spirit chooses in real time as the "rhema" song. It is always the rhema song or **song of the time** that does the job, and God knows why; therefore you must train yourself to hear from God about the **song of the time**. In order not to disappoint God therefore, study to show yourself approved (2 Timothy 2:15), to correctly divide between the repertoire of rehearsed songs (the songs you already know) and the **song of the time** (the song of the Spirit – the song which God wants to use or minister at that particular moment) because the "rhema" song is what can accomplish the purpose of God for the hour, and will certainly not return void.

Sometimes the **song of the time** may not be known at all, and can be a new song that breaks forth expressly from the Holy Spirit; so the worship leader, soloist or lead vocalist should train themselves to be a composer, and should know about instant reception and instant delivery, or how to compose a fresh song straight from the God's throne in heaven (Revelation 4:1–11); the instrumentalists should also know how to do the same and/or accompany accordingly, because the fresh song can begin with the instrumentalist(s); whoever God chooses to initiate the fresh song, the rest should know how to accompany; sometimes the composition can be in sequence because God can choose multiple composers on the same stage, and each one has to know their turn to deliver, just as Paul gave orderly guidance for manifestations of spiritual gifts (1 Corinthians 14:28–33). Ephesians 5:19 and

Colossians 3:16 tell us that there are psalms and hymns (the songs we already know or have rehearsed) and spiritual songs (the rhema songs, including those which we have never heard before and can break out as fresh songs from the throne in heaven) which we can refer to as the **songs of the time.**

When an act of praise is prophetically inspired

When God gives a specific direction, as in the examples of Jehoshaphat (2 Chronicles 20:21–23) and Jericho (Joshua 6) – to go into the battle with the prescribed action of praise, that was prophetic praise.

Equally, when someone puts up an act as inspired by the Holy Spirit, for example, a dance, or when an instrumentalist ministers by their instrument (whether the drum, guitar or tambourine) in a way that they understand not to be natural to them, this act of praise can be prophetic, and of specific edification to that congregation or even the entire body of Christ if the ministration can be interpreted. Technically, some vessels may receive that ministration spiritually, depending on how well-tuned they are, or on what spiritual frequency they are operating, but others may miss out on the frequency and it would take the interpretation of the ministration to convey the edification to all. Then also, God by His own sovereignty may want to have the interpretation vocalized, to set into motion His will and purposes, so that the original prophetic ministration is not voided, and for His word or direction to be accomplished (Isaiah 55:11).

Chapter 7

Dancing in Church

Key Texts

- ✓ Psalm 149:3
- ✓ 2 Samuel 6:14–22
- ✓ Hebrews 12:22–24
- ✓ Romans 12:2
- ✓ 1 Corinthians 12:10
- ✓ 1 Corinthians 14:13

If you take a look across the globe, you would realize that in some cultures, dancing is not predominant in church services, whereas it is predominant in others. We must first establish the point that dancing is biblical. Psalm 149:3 states: "Let them praise his name with dancing and make music to him with tambourine and harp." There are many other scriptures that command worshipers to dance in church. We must also establish another point – that dancing is not always the "holy" act - it does not take place in the Holy Place or the Holy of Holies; it takes place in the courtyard. Earlier in Chapter 2, we established the point that dancing has no formula. As dancing may not be a "holy" act, it can offend onlookers, or come across as indecent to others, but not necessarily to God. So we need to be very careful how we judge someone else's dancing, and leave the judging to God. 2 Samuel 6:14 states that "David, wearing a linen ephod, danced before the LORD with all his might" and Michal was offended by it. The ephod is like a waist coat, and could be slightly below hip level at the longest. It is usually worn over other vestments. But as it was linen, and also very short, if that is all what David was wearing (without other vestments), then obviously David would have been exposed to non-intimate others while he danced vigorously in such a costume. 2 Samuel 6:16 states that "when she [Michal] saw King David leaping and dancing before the LORD, she despised him in her heart." So the jealous Michal who was David's lover accosted him and began to tease and complain: "How glorious was the king of Israel today, uncovering himself today in the eyes of the maids of his servants, as one of the base fellows shamelessly uncovers himself!" (2 Samuel 6:20). David then retorted in his zeal for God: "It was before the LORD, who chose me instead of your father and all his house, to appoint me ruler over the people of the LORD, over Israel. Therefore I will play music before the LORD and I will become even more undignified than this, and I will be humble in my own sight. But as for the maidservants of whom you have spoken, by them I will be held in honor" (2 Samuel 6:21–22). Hence, you should try to deal with yourself if someone's dancing offends you, and leave the rest to God. It is not clear whether David had misjudged the jealousy of his lover or whether he had over-reacted, but that just goes to show that human emotions can be fraught with imperfection.

One may argue that, if a believer is already in the throne room or before the Lord so to speak, and their dancing is a bodily expression of what their inner man is saying, then they are dancing in the spirit. This may be true, however, please note that your spirit may be born-again and perfect (Hebrews 12:23), but your body is not born-again, and therefore cannot be guaranteed to manifest spirit, but flesh. Furthermore, your soul (mind, feelings and emotions) which processes your actions from your inner man to your body isn't born-again either, and therefore cannot be guaranteed to process spirit or perfection. Therefore contamination and perversion can influence what your inner man wants to express and how your body expresses your inner man. This simply means that apart from your spirit, your soul and body cannot be guaranteed to act perfectly because these elements of your personality are not born-again; Romans 12:2 says that we are being transformed by the renewing of our minds. Human beings are not angels who were created in such a way that their whole beings worship God perfectly, and the onlooker might be perceiving from an imperfect point of view. However, this is not an excuse for believers to deliberately dance indecently in the church. Yet who am I to judge! We must leave the judging to the One who can judge all dancing in church or elsewhere, and whether by Christians or non-Christians, because you never know what their inner spirit may be communicating in real time. Hebrews 12:23 states: "... You have come to God the Judge of all, to the spirits of just men made perfect."

If there is not sufficient space at the meeting place, then dancing would infringe on others, however space is a practical issue which each meeting and congregation have to grapple with, depending on the arrangement of space available at the meeting place. Space is not a biblical issue. But please note the point that dancing before the Lord has no formula.

Dancing in church can be prophetic sometimes, for example: (a) when someone dances under an anointing of the Holy Spirit whether they understand so or not; or (b) when someone dances in a way that they understand not to be natural to them. However, just as speaking in diverse tongues (1 Corinthians 12:10) without interpretation does not edify anyone (1 Corinthians 14:13), so it is that prophetic dancing may not edify if no one can interpret it. I must point out that Augustine preferred hymns and songs to dancing because he thought only the lyrics of hymns and songs were articulate and could edify, whereas he viewed dancing as inarticulate and therefore could not provide edification. However, dancing, especially prophetic dancing, can articulate a message, and therefore can also edify. In other words, dancing can speak. One has to wonder though, if Augustine thought that the dancing he witnessed in church spoke nothing or was inarticulate, why did he detest it so much? Just what did the dancing communicate to his emotions which caused offence, whatever the offence was?

Dancing in church has caused offence and controversy over time, and has in some respects become a stumbling block in the church or body of Christ instead of it fulfilling Psalm 149:3. Throughout church history, some leaders who could not stand the dance of certain congregants – whether because of their weaknesses, prejudices, or misunderstandings – have taken ecclesiastical positions against dancing in church. The result is that church dancing across the globe has assumed a cultural, racial and continental divide, and congregants in some cultures feel free to dance in church, whereas others do not. The full detail of how this occurred, and the influence of Augustine on church dancing, are captured in my paper.[1]

---

[1] Amoah, Michael. "Christian Musical Worship and 'Hostility to the Body': The Medieval Influence Versus the Pentecostal Revolution." *Implicit Religion* 7 (2004): 59-75.

Chapter 8

The Ministry of the Minstrel

Key Texts

- ✓ 2 Kings 3:14–17
- ✓ Exodus 15:1–21
- ✓ Ephesians 4:11
- ✓ 1 Chronicles 9:33
- ✓ Numbers 12:1–16
- ✓ 1 Samuel 10:5–13
- ✓ 1 Samuel 19:20
- ✓ 1 Chronicles 15 & 16
- ✓ 1 Chronicles 25:2
- ✓ 2 Chronicles 20
- ✓ 1 Kings 12:15–17
- ✓ 2 Kings 3
- ✓ Ezra 3:10
- ✓ 1 Corinthians 14
- ✓ Luke 4:18–19

A minstrel as called by God to minister in the Holy Spirit is an itinerant psalmist or musician with an apostolic mantle to minister or deliver the **song of the time**: (a) to create a path in the spiritual realm for the word of the Lord to be released and received; (b) to usher, connect or link up a congregation, group or an individual into a move of the Holy Spirit; (c) to break through for the works of God to be done. Three examples of this calling found in the Bible are:

1. Miriam the older sister of Moses. Her instrument was the tambourine or timbrel (Exodus 15:20).
2. The minstrel who ministered before Elisha could prophesy in 2 Kings 3:15.
3. A group of minstrels under the tutelage of Samuel the prophet, who Saul encountered to confirm his calling after he was anointed by Samuel the prophet (1 Samuel 10:5). They had a stringed instrument, a tambourine, a flute, and a harp.

The choice of instrument for the minstrel is a matter for God and them. For example, they could be a timbrelist, flutist, harpist, trumpeter, lyrist, piper, pianist, guitarist, saxophonist, violinist, or percussionists such as cymbalists, drummers, congalists, and bongolists, whatever the case may be.

The secular minstrel

Before we delve deep into the calling of a minstrel, let us establish who they are naturally or secularly, just to put it in context. I should also say that the ministry and activity of the minstrel have been occurring long before our modern languages, however as I do not live in the Bible lands (Palestine, Egypt and Asia Minor), my examples of the minstrel will come from the countries in which I have lived – England and Ghana. Nevertheless, the definition of who is a secular minstrel would suffice elsewhere in the world. According to Wikipedia, the natural or secular minstrel is simply an orator or poet who is also a musician, and can entertain or deliver messages and tales of real or imaginary historical events through music, with harps, fiddles, bagpipes, flutes, flageolets, citterns and kettledrums such as were the common instruments in medieval England. They are always itinerant, roaming or operating from place to place, and from event to event, whether it is a feast, festival or concert, individually or in group. They always had a mission to accomplish: their performances had to be catchy, trendy, or appropriate to the mood of the places they visited. Originally, they roamed or had no settled abode, and earned their keep from their itinerant performances. Modern minstrels may be karaoke or buskers. The key selling point about minstrels is how they accomplished their mission or delivered an entertainment or performance so that the audience always proclaimed that it was worth attending. It may sound trivial, but because minstrels earned their keep from a satisfactory audience, they made a lot of effort to know in advance the background of the towns and villages where they performed, or the historical and wartime context of the time, so that the tale or story they sang either chimed with their folklore or acted as a message of hope during wartime. From that background research, they also got to know what tunes to play to capture the time and mood of the towns or events at which they performed. The more successful ones who knew the history and folklore performed at king's palaces, and also became jesters. With time, minstrels' galleries became part of the palace complex, for example, the Great Hall of Durham Castle at University College Durham, which was once used for entertainment by the Prince Bishops. As the tradition of minstrels got attracted to the church, some very few cathedrals were constructed to have minstrels' galleries, such as Exeter Cathedral. But the performers here were not necessarily allowed to perform in the church services. There is a possibility that minstrels operated at the courtyard of the Jewish temple in biblical times, because Psalm 100:4 states: "enter his gates with thanksgiving and into his courts with praise."

The Christian minstrel

Let us now establish some key points about one who is called by God to be a minstrel to the church or the body of Christ. First, minstrels are always prophets – and this comes with the calling. Miriam was a prophetess (Ex 15:20). The minstrel has to pick up the **song of the time**, and the calling of the prophet(ess) is necessary. Some spiritual characteristics of serious minstrels include that they live under an open heaven, hence their reception is instant and accurate, and explains why they can easily hear from God or pick up the **song of the time** when everyone else is not in tune, confused, distressed, or does not know what to do. Because they are used to living under an open heaven, it is also easy for them to know if there are interferences in the spiritual realm, and discern with pinpoint accuracy what manner of interference there is, as well as how to deal with it. Indeed it is precisely their ability to deal with or handle the spiritual realm, and of course their ability to live under an open heaven, which enables minstrels to:

a. create a path in the spiritual realm for the word of the Lord to be released and received;
b. usher, connect or link up a congregation, group or an individual into a move of the Holy Spirit, and;
3. break through for the works of God to be done, as I originally set out at the beginning of this chapter.

Second, they have a mission to accomplish at each event that God ordains they should minister. The minstrel always carries an apostolic mantle – this is necessary to deliver the mission for which they have been sent. This does not necessarily make them an apostle (as in the fivefold ministry listed in Ephesians 4:11), however some minstrels may be called by God as apostles in their own right of calling. An apostle is a "sent one" or simply one who has been sent – to accomplish a mission of course. The ministry of the minstrel is apostolic because there is a sense of mission about it, in that, you have to break the ground for the event at which you are going to minister, and you must fulfil the mission for which you have been sent there to minister; there is a key point about this particular aspect of the ministry of the minstrel, which I will make later in the course of this chapter. The minstrel can minister without playing their own instrument if they can obtain musical accompaniment from some other musician(s) – most likely someone who can play the minstrel's instrument that s/he likes the most, and furthermore if this backing instrumentalist knows how to minister before the Lord. The minstrel can also minister without external musical accompaniment – their instrument(s) should be playing in their spirit as they minister, and if they are well trained or well equipped, they should be able to follow that musical accompaniment from within.

Third, minstrels are very devoted to their ministry. The Bible states in 1 Chronicles 9:33 that some of them "... lodged in the chambers, and were free from other duties; for they were employed in that work day and night." This devotion or separation unto the Lord keeps them in constant fellowship with the Holy Spirit who is their guide. The Bible also states in 1 Chronicles 25:1 that minstrels were separated unto the service for which they were called to render. They were separated or devoted to "prophesy with harps, stringed instruments and cymbals."

Two examples of accomplished minstrels in the church or body of Christ, both of whose callings I have directly benefited from, and one of whom I have understudied, are Mary Ghansah of Ghana, and Graham Kendrick of England. Graham reads and writes music, and plays the guitar and keyboard. He is very unassuming, and worships at a relatively small Baptist church near Greenwich, London (as per the last time I recall). Mary plays the guitar and keyboard, and has many recorded and published compositions to her career, just as Graham. Mary also founded Open Heavens Ministry, of which I was a member. Two further examples of minstrels are Susan Turner of England, and Elijah Saforo of Ghana. Susan is a Salvationist who used to worship at Staines Corp in England. One of her instruments is the tambourine. Together with a team of songsters Susan trained, they have performed at various events across the United Kingdom and abroad; I once attended an evening concert by Susan and her group in Regent Hall, the Salvation Army Corps at Oxford Street in London, where I fellowshiped from October 1990 before making my way to Action Chapel. Regent Hall Corps is a very musical church in their own right, with three services on a Sunday; the afternoon indoor meeting is predominantly musical, and it is a regular Sunday feature for the Regent Hall band to perform outside Oxford Circus underground station and be a Christian witness between the afternoon indoor musical and the evening indoor meeting. Many random visitors on Oxford Street have encountered Jesus that way, and have followed the band indoors for the evening meeting; and many have given their lives to the Lord. Vinesong Ministries led by John Watson is also a minstrel group.

The ministry of the minstrel is prophetic and apostolic. However, as in all forms of ministry, the levels of operation vary according to each minister's grace, calling, experience, and to what extent they have studied before God to show themselves approved.

Miriam the minstrel

Miriam the minstrel, with a tambourine, led the **song of the time** which Moses and the people of Israel sang when God delivered them out of the red sea. The song began like this: "I will sing to the Lord, for He has triumphed gloriously! The horse and the rider He has cast into the sea!" (Exodus 15:1 or 15:20). Many other famous and longstanding songs within the church or body of Christ have come out of the lyrics in Exodus 15. For example: (a) "the Lord is my strength and song, and He has become my salvation" (Exodus 15:2); or (b) "Who is like You, O Lord, among the gods? Who is like You, glorious in holiness, fearful in praises, doing wonders?" (Exodus 15:11). Because Miriam was a prophetess, she was able to pick up the song from the realm of the Spirt, and as a minstrel, she had no trouble leading the song prophetically, until the full song was brought to completion when it did. Because of Miriam's rare gift and calling as a minstrel and a prophetess, and how useful she was to the people of Israel, Moses took the trouble to intercede for her to be restored, after she was struck with leprosy (Numbers 12:1–16). Being Moses's sister was just coincidence, it was her rare calling as a minstrel that really mattered to Moses. As a leper, Miriam would have been excluded from the main body of Israel and automatically from her priestly duties as a minstrel. Moses obviously realized that if he lost Miriam's gift and calling, it would take a generation to raise another minstrel such as Miriam, who was also that close to him. Therefore Moses interceded for her restoration. The training process for a minstrel takes time, and is very unique to God, minstrel by minstrel. Hence minstrels are very few and far between. When they come your way, treat them very well and with respect, because if you lose them or maltreat them, you may have to wait a long time, sometimes a generation, to be allocated another one; you may not even be reallocated another.

Elisha's minstrel

As already explained, minstrels are itinerant by trade. Because the minstrel was itinerant he/she had to be fetched, hence Elisha said "bring me a minstrel" (2 Kings 3:15) as opposed to the resident psalmist or musician (e.g., Jahaziel) who would already have been with Jehoshaphat's troops while they were encamped at the battlefield with Jehoshaphat. Please note that the war machine which accompanied the King consisted of not just soldiers, but other professionals such as prophets, priests, psalmists, servants, cooks, footmen, and spies who handled no weapons at all. When the ministry of resident psalmists was first established by King David, Asaph was the head of the prophetic music wing of the Levitic priesthood (1 Chronicles 16:5). He also became the private prophet to David (1 Chronicles 25:2) and scripted many chapters in the Book of Psalms. Other examples of resident psalmists are Benaiah and Jahaziel (1 Chronicles 16:6). It was Jahaziel the resident psalmist and prophet through whom God spoke to King Jehoshaphat before the famous battle with the Moabites, Ammonites, and the inhabitants of Mount Seir (2 Chronicles

20:14-17). Please note that as Jahaziel was resident, and part of the King's entourage (and not itinerant), he didn't have to be fetched, he simply performed his duty on the spot as one of the resident Levitic prophets when the Spirit of the Lord came upon him (2 Chronicles 20:13-14). Miriam would have had no trouble at all keeping up with the itinerary of Moses and the people of Israel, who as we know, were very peripatetic in their history. The Bible offers no clues about the lyrics or ministration the minstrel ministered for Elisha the prophet, other than that s/he accomplished the mission, because the hand of the Lord came upon Elisha when s/he ministered, and the word of the Lord was released for King Jehoshaphat.

It is important to set out some brief background to the appearance and ministry of Elisha's minstrel. As David was himself a prophet and did not want to miss out on divine instructions (1 Chronicles 15:13), he had special regard for the Levitic priesthood, and established the order which set aside time to wait upon God for special instructions (1 Chronicles 15:11-15). In this order, he further established the prophetic music wing (1 Chronicles 15:16 to 1 Chronicles 16:6). When the kingdom of Israel became split into north and south during the time of King Rehoboam (1 Kings 12:15-17), the southern Kingdom led by the house of David with its capital in Judah retained the prophetic Levitic priesthood in its pristine state, but the prophetic ministry of the idolatrous northern kingdom became polluted with false prophets whom Jehoshaphat the King of Judah could not trust. Therefore when Jehoshaphat had to team up with the northern King Jehoram against the Moabites, Elisha had to be summoned, to break the tradition of relying on the polluted team of joint false prophets (2 Kings 3). When Elisha arrived on the scene, he also asked for a minstrel to be summoned. Both Jehoshaphat and Elisha had tasted of the requirements of the pristine prophetic musical order established by David (Ezra 3:10), and knew exactly what to do. We must understand that it is no idle talk that David established the ministry of praise and worship; the Bible states that he himself made or invented instruments (Amos 6:5 / 2 Chronicles 7:6 / 1 Chronicles 23:5 / 2 Chronicles 29:27). It appears that David was very engrossed in music. No wonder that he committed what has been considered as a gross act in dancing and didn't care (2 Samuel 6:14–23). One has to be gross in order to be engrossed; also interpreted to mean that operating at maximum devotion to your calling can get you engrossed in your calling.

Samuel's minstrels (manifestations in praise and worship)

Miriam had a band following her, with dancing (Exodus 15:20). Because of the prophetic nature of the ministry of the minstrel, sometimes they moved together as a band of prophets from place to place (itinerant). We know from 1 Samuel 10:5 that Saul met a band of itinerant prophets with string instrument, tambourine, flute and harp, and they were prophesying; they were minstrels. Their mission was to create a realm of operation for Saul to encounter, that will release Saul into his calling and turn him into another man – the King of Israel (1 Samuel 10:6). Because this band of prophets knew their job, they had already prepared the spiritual realm; and as soon as Saul reached their presence (or entered that realm), reception was instant, the Spirit of God came upon Saul, and he prophesied among them. They accomplished their mission (1 Samuel 10:10) in the exact manner as was prophesied by Samuel the prophet (1 Samuel 10:5–6). The Bible states that this band of prophetic minstrels were under the tutelage of Samuel the prophet (1 Samuel 19:20), and it happened subsequently with this band of prophets who knew their mission and their job, that three separate groups of messengers sent by Saul encountered the band, and automatically entered into prophetic trances (1 Samuel 19:20–21).

We have already established the point that dancing can be in the flesh sometimes. But let us now deal with what is not in the flesh, or what is spiritual. The minstrel will recognize a dance if it is prophetic, and can interpret the act or ministration (as discussed in Chapter 6 on Prophetic Praise and Chapter 7 on Dancing in Church). The minstrel will also recognize if a musical instrument is playing prophetically, and can interpret the ministration whether or not the instrumentalist knows they are playing prophetically. Please note that it is almost improbable for such manifestations to occur in a normal church meeting unless the person leading the meeting carries the mantle of a minstrel (under which such manifestations do often occur), or unless someone else in the meeting carries the mantle of a minstrel and agrees (with God) for the unction upon their life to impact on that meeting – based on the principle that "the spirits of the prophets are subject to the prophets" (1 Corinthians 14:32). Even so, whoever is leading the meeting should know this and understand operations, or be mindful of the potential contribution from the other minstrel present in that meeting (if the one leading the meeting is not a minstrel), or s/he can miss the anointing or potential contribution from this other minstrel present, whether this other minstrel is on stage or just in the congregation. If led by the Holy Spirit, the one leading the meeting can request the other minstrel present to come and minister, and if that minstrel is flowing and willing to minister, s/he would be of benefit to the meeting; as already mentioned, "the spirits of the prophets are subject to the prophets" (1 Corinthians 14:32). Outside these parameters, if God wants to initiate or stir up prophetic giftings by His own sovereignty, that is another matter. However, just as speaking in diverse tongues (1 Corinthians 12:10) without interpretation does not edify anyone (1 Corinthians 14:13), so it is that prophetic instrumentation and prophetic dancing may not edify if no one can interpret it. Their manifestations may even apply in spiritual warfare, and can be useful in that regard. However, the manifestations may not edify if none can interpret. Hence Paul who was not a singer wished that believers were able to prophesy or interpret rather than just manifesting something spiritual (1 Corinthians 14:5).

Indeed, Paul went on to explain specifically, that if the prophetic instrumentation could not be interpreted, it was of no edification to anyone (1 Corinthians 14:7–8). One has to wonder how and why Paul gave this word even though he was not a singer; he was not ignorant; he had revelation! If any minister does not understand what is manifesting, or is not trained to do so, it is better for the body of Christ that they do not attempt to interfere, or interpret. The Bible states that "if anyone is ignorant, let him be ignorant" (1 Corinthians 14:38).

We therefore have to admit to ourselves that confusion about the manifestations of spiritual gifts in church, in what order and their interpretation, especially during worship and prayer, had become a problem which Paul decided to deal with; and that is why Paul set out the guidance for the order of manifestations of gifts in church or in Christian gatherings (1 Corinthians 14:26–40). As usual, the worshipers and prayer warriors among the congregation were competing with their spiritual gifts, and someone had to resolve the issue or shape them up. But Paul was not ignorant even though he was not a singer, and fully understood the role of worship in church and the value of the music, so he did not throw the baby away with the bath water, and highlighted the role of music/worship and instruments in prayer or spiritual warfare, and the prophetic aspects of worship in his guidance for prophesying in church. In verses 7 and 8, Paul stated:

- Even things without life, whether flute or harp, when they make a sound, unless they make a distinction in the sounds, how will it be known what is piped or played? [8] For if the trumpet makes an uncertain sound, who will prepare for battle? (1 Corinthians 14:7–8).

It is therefore absolutely vital to skillfully manage vain attempts to prophesy by individuals from any part of the congregation, because these actions can be distractions to the corporate move of the Holy Spirit, and can even mislead the meeting, to say the least. As much as possible, the meeting should be guided and led from the pulpit because God is not the author of confusion (1 Corinthians 14:33), and whoever is leading from the pulpit must have knowledge, and also understand operations, as explained above. But this just emphasizes the point, that the body of Christ must believe God for the office of the minstrel, because it is extremely necessary. A minstrel will cover for all the scenarios and operations already explained, and if a minstrel is in charge, you have no cause to worry. If you do not have a minstrel in your congregation, you are missing something, and if you have not encountered a minstrel in your generation, you have missed something. The office of the minstrel is perhaps the principal means by which the church can experience or benefit from the full plethora of gifts and callings that manifested with the minstrels in the Bible, and particularly with the band of prophets who were trained by Samuel. If God does not raise such a one who can train or oversee such manifestations, how can we experience the best of worship? It also means that we must respect who minstrels are, and not stifle them because of ministerial insecurities. God is the giver of the gift. When a minstrel is in charge, everything will be done decently and in order (1 Corinthians 14:40). In the same vein, if an ignorant or incompetent person is overseeing the meeting, they will not know what to do, and the chances are that the anointing will not be generated for those rare and much needed manifestations, because only the minstrel carries the anointing for that kind of business, and everyone else would have missed God or missed out on the occasion just because of ignorance or ministerial insecurities. It is not for nothing that the Bible states: "My people are destroyed for **lack of knowledge**. Because you have rejected knowledge, I also will reject you from being priest for Me; Because you have forgotten the law of your God, I also will forget your children" (Hosea 4:6).

I should point out that dancing and interpretation under the influence of music and rhythm have been perverted by satan and do manifest in all cultures in various ways; whether covertly in the natural, or overtly by satanic agents - they are both deceptive and a perversion of the real and original gifts from God. For example, a fetish priest can perform a dance under a demonic influence and the interpretation of the dance becomes the message or oracle from the gods. But this is not from God, and certainly not as genuine as what God ordained to manifest in 1 Samuel 10 and 1 Samuel 19 as already explained in this chapter; one must study these portions of scripture in detail.

In another dimension, especially in contemporary Christianity, it has become fashionable for secularly trained dancers to express the worship, sometimes with flag-waving gestures, and sometimes without that. These can be judged as natural gestures, and may not be attributed serious spiritual significance; they are certainly not comparable to what occurred in 1 Samuel 10 and 1 Samuel 19. So now we know why God takes his time to groom minstrels, because there can be a lot of room for deception and counterfeit.

Among other things, the manifestation of the ministry of the minstrel is rare because: (a) God doesn't call many people into it; (b) not many called are prepared to pay the price for the calling; (c) God will not send a minstrel to a ministry that is not prepared to host the calling; (d) many ministers and ministries cannot identify a minstrel for who they are, or when they do, are not prepared to accommodate and make room for them; (e) some ministries do not understand the operations of the calling and therefore do not know what to do with minstrels – they can frustrate the calling innocently or deliberately; (f) some ministers and ministries feel very insecure with minstrels; (g) most minstrels who know their calling will not manifest it until they locate a place where there is an opportunity to manifest it, or until they locate a ministry with sufficient knowledge that is prepared to accept the manifestation and calling of the minstrel.

Check points about the Minstrel

The calling of the minstrel is very beautiful when it is manifesting, and many people try, or have tried to be so, even if they are not. The calling of a minstrel to the body of Christ cannot be faked, and the following check points are useful:

- If you claim to be a minstrel to the body of Christ, but you are not a prophet, then you are not.
- If you claim to be a minstrel to the body of Christ, but do not understand what is meant by the **song of the time**, or do not know how to pick up the **song of the time**, then you are not.
- If you claim to be a minstrel to the body of Christ, but cannot recognize when an instrument is playing prophetically, or make out what an instrument is saying when a prophetic ministration is taking place, then you are not.
- If you claim to be a minstrel to the body of Christ, but do not know how to operate apostolically in the spiritual realm, then you are not. If you do not understand what I mean by this, then consider yourself not.
- If you claim to be a minstrel to the body of Christ, but do not know what your instrument is, then you are not. You do not have to be an expert at playing that

instrument, but that is the instrument which ignites your spirit, and you must know which instrument it is, or you are not. You don't have to play that instrument yourself at functions; another musician can play it for you, or even your spirit can play that instrument for you and you would hear it in your spirit; but you must know the instrument, or you are not.

- You do not become a minstrel to the body of Christ just because you can organize, or have organized an itinerant schedule for yourself. If God has not sent you to those places, then you don't have a mission, and won't know what to do when you get there. You may perform something there, and even receive a loud applause, but it would be vanity, because God had not sent you. Minstrels therefore carry a huge responsibility as to which invitations they must (not) honor or accept, so that the calling is not abused. If the source of the invitation does not know how to handle the ministry of a minstrel, then you must certainly not honor the invitation because the wo/ man of God won't know what to preach once you've broken through for him/her, and your calling would have been abused; this is the key point which I referred to earlier in this chapter, that I would make in the course of the chapter.

- A minstrel may not tutor another person as a protégé (just because they can sing or play an instrument) unless you are absolutely certain that the trainee is called by God as a minstrel, and that it is specifically you that God has ordained to train this fellow, otherwise you will be casting pearls to swine. You may give them all the coaching that you can muster, and they will still not manifest the calling if God has not called them into it. The minstrel must establish from God that the protégé / trainee must come under their tutelage.

- If you recognize that you are called to be a minstrel, then ask the Holy Spirit to train you Himself, and He will surely organize that. God may also orchestrate for you to meet an experienced minstrel that He has ordained for you to understudy.

- That said, the ministry of the minstrel is not for the fun to create an atmosphere for believers to bask in the glory of God and do nothing with it as in most musical concerts. More importantly, the ministry of the minstrel is to enable direction to come forth, prepare the grounds and play a leading role in the ministry of saving souls, to operate to bring deliverance to both the churched and unchurched, and release blessings to humanity. If the principal aim of any Christian event is to win souls, bring deliverance to captives, or wait on God for specific direction or blessing, then you have the minstrels to use. That is what the anointing is for. Jesus said in Luke 4:18–19 that:

> The Spirit of the LORD is upon Me, because He has anointed Me to preach the gospel to the poor; He has sent Me to heal the brokenhearted, to

proclaim liberty to the captives and recovery of sight to the blind, to set at liberty those who are oppressed; to proclaim the acceptable year of the LORD.

- If a church, musical group, or the body of Christ is low on evangelistic drive and deliverance, that is one of a variety of reasons why the minstrels are not showing forth. Indeed minstrels can engineer the drive and lead the way, or even be principal actors, but the clergy better be prepared for the minstrels, and be seen to be demonstrating that strong drive and vision towards saving souls, bringing deliverance to the captives, and seeking God for direction. Then there would be a clear purpose, appetite and space for the minstrels, otherwise the minstrels would have wasted their effort and time, and God's time.

Chapter 9

Worship and Deliverance

Key Texts

- ✓ 1 Samuel 16:14–23
- ✓ 1 Samuel 17:15
- ✓ 1 Samuel 10:5–13
- ✓ 1 Samuel 19:20
- ✓ Luke 4:18

We have already discussed in Chapter 5 that music is good for therapy. We also know that this is not some modern discovery. We learn from the Bible that when King Saul was in torment, the staff in the king's palace did not recommend a massage. Instead, they suggested to find him a psalmist, knowing that the music from the psalmist can deliver therapy and heal his soul. The ministration from psalmistry or minstrelsy was already a well-known and well-practised form of remedy. Based on the job description and the person specification required, David met the criteria, and was head-hunted for the role (1 Sam 16:14–22). We know from verse 23 that when David played his instrument (harp/lyre), Saul was refreshed and relieved.

Let us diagnose the spirituality of the sequence of events. The Bible makes it clear that Saul was troubled by a distressing spirit (verse 14); that the musician was required to minister when the distressing spirit manifested (verse 16); and that the ministration from the psalmist would bring relief from the distressing spirit (verse 16). We already know (from Chapter 5) about the therapy which music can bring to emotions, and that music was sought for Saul's therapy, but music alone is not enough to dispel a demonic or distressing spirit. In the first place, this distressing spirit came about because the Spirit of the Lord had departed from Saul; and the distressing sprit was from the Lord (1 Samuel 16:14 & 23). Hence it takes only God Himself or His Holy Spirit to displace or replace this distressing spirit; it can also be interpreted that it is the anointing that breaks the yoke. In this instance, because David was an anointed psalmist, the presence of the Lord came along with his ministration, and this anointing displaced or replaced the distressing spirit, and Saul became refreshed (1 Samuel 16:23). It is also just like the presence of God that was carried by the band of prophets trained by Samuel the prophet, who knew how to prepare and maintain a spiritual realm of open heaven for God to operate, so that whoever encountered their presence or had the privilege of entering that realm of presence, entered into a prophetic trance and began to prophesy (1 Samuel 10:5–13 & 1 Samuel 19:20). Hence fellowshiping with the Holy Spirit through worship, is a means of receiving deliverance from demonic spirits. But this may not eliminate the root of the problem.

Unless God by His sovereignty intervenes directly and restores fully, or that the root of the problem is addressed by intercession – whether by worship and/or the laying on of hands by anointed ministers (Luke 4:18), the distressing spirit would come back as soon as the anointing lifts. We know (from 1 Sam 17:15; 18:10; and 19:9) that David returned to minister to King Saul on a few more occasions, meaning that each time David departed from Saul, the anointing of the Holy Spirit departed with David, and the distressing spirit resumed its position with Saul. In other words, the refreshing from the Holy Spirit brought Saul some relief (or temporary deliverance) which disappeared once David departed.

We also know that Paul the Apostle encountered a similar problem (of torment from an evil spirit) which he described as a thorn in the flesh that was given to him, or a messenger of satan to buffet him (2 Corinthians 12:7). When Paul cried to God for deliverance, God told him that "my grace is sufficient for you, for My strength is made perfect in weakness" (2 Corinthians 12:7–9). So we need the intervention of God whether to survive in the situation or to be delivered. Whatever your situation might be, you can plead with God to deliver or restore you. But if you need advice or help, you must not hesitate to approach trusted and experienced ministers; it may be that prayer from ministers, or the prayer of the saints, should be sufficient for your deliverance.

Chapter 10

Worshipers before God regularly

Key Texts

- ✓ 1 Chronicles 9:33
- ✓ 1 Chronicles 6:32
- ✓ 1 Chronicles 15 & 16
- ✓ 1 Chronicles 25:2
- ✓ 2 Chronicles 20
- ✓ 2 Kings 3:15
- ✓ Ezra 3:10

We have discussed the benefits of worshiping, and spending time before the Lord. The more you do this, the more intimate your relationship with God will become. For those who are called into the ministry of praise and worship, and particularly those who are worship leaders, it is imperative that you minister before the Lord regularly, daily, all the time. The Bible states in 1 Chronicles 9:33 that they "... lodged in the chambers, and were free from other duties; for they were employed in that work day and night." Indeed your very life on this earth must be a walk before the Lord, even if the minstrel is not in full-time ministry or does not earn their livelihood from their instrument. Because the minstrel is before the Lord day and night, they are able to know (from the Lord) what song to minister, or how to minister (before the Lord) on their instrument to bring the breakthrough. The Bible states in 1 Chronicles 6:32 that "they were ministering with music before the dwelling place of the tabernacle of meeting, until Solomon had built the house of the Lord in Jerusalem, and they served in their office according to their order."

In 1 Chronicles 16, David appointed a selection of the Levites who worshipped before the Ark of the Covenant; these were all resident psalmists or musicians, and were also prophets. Asaph was the head of this special musical and prophetic wing of the Levitic priesthood, and you will find in the Book of Psalms that a good number of the psalms had been scripted by Asaph, who was also a private prophet to King David (1 Chronicles 25:2). Where David himself scripted the psalm, or if he did not minister it himself, then Asaph would have been the first custodian of it and would be given instructions on what to do with it. The Bible states in 1 Chronicles 16:7 and following, that "… David first delivered this psalm into the hand of Asaph and his brethren, to thank the Lord …." In this very prophetic musical wing, Benaiah and Jahaziel are particularly singled out as resident priests who regularly ministered with trumpets before the Ark (1 Chronicles 16:6). It was Jahaziel through whom God spoke to King Jehoshaphat before they embarked on the onslaught against the Moabites, Ammonites, and the inhabitants of Mount Seir (2 Chronicles 20:14–17). As he was a resident psalmist and part of the King's entourage, he did not need to be "fetched" like the minstrel of 2 Kings 3:15 who was itinerant and was not with King Jehoshaphat's entourage on the battlefield.

Once a church has been founded or set up, it is useful to have a worship department made up of singers and psalmists who would stand in their calling and support that church – an order that was established by David. The Bible states in Ezra 3:10 that "When the builders laid the foundation of the temple of the Lord, the priests stood in their apparel with trumpets, and the Levites, the sons of Asaph, with cymbals, to praise the Lord, according to the ordinance of David king of Israel." The church should also locate a minstrel, for as and when s/he might be needed, as would be led by the Holy Spirit from time to time.

Chapter 11

Dressing as an act of Worship

Key Texts

- ✓ 1 Kings 8
- ✓ Matthew 6:27–29
- ✓ 2 Corinthians 11:14

As Christians, we walk before God, so dressing and the way you carry yourself about is an act of worship, and we need to be mindful how we do it. We have the ability to be creative, but this must not be abused. Particularly for those called into the ministry of praise and worship, something about the gifting and calling of a worshiper causes you to dream, or receive from God the ability to be creative, especially in the way to dress, and one has to be careful not to abuse this creativity. Unbelievers in the music industry have perverted this gift and can dress very inappropriately. But the Church must not copy this. In simple terms, believers should not "dress to kill". Solomon was one great worshiper in the Bible (1 Kings 8) and used to dress flamboyantly. But your dressing can be vanity if it is inappropriate or does not worship or honor God. Matthew 6:27–29 states: "And why do you worry about clothes? See how the lilies of the field grow. They do not labor or spin. Yet I tell you that not even Solomon in all his splendor was dressed like one of these."

Our outfit may reflect our "infit" or the state of our inner man, or emotions, and rightly so, just as we dress according to the occasion for weddings or funerals, whether attending to rejoice or to mourn respectively. Formality may also dictate the attire, as in choir uniforms, school uniforms, military uniforms, or any other uniform. But we need to be cautious about ritualistic or symbolic dressing for the purpose of depicting spiritual things, because we are no longer in the Old Testament, and the Holy Spirit has liberated us, and can liberate further. Some religious leaders prescribe all-white outfit to depict purity or holiness, even though the whiteness of your attire does not guarantee or depict holiness. We need to be careful about such directions because the "white garment" sects began that way. A clergyman in London devoted one Sunday each month just for worship. For the first Sunday of this program, he prescribed an all-white outfit to be worn, on the basis that when God gave him the revelation for the program, he saw everyone dressed in white, and worshiping God in holiness and purity. The all-white dress code was prescribed for subsequent monthly worship events, and this soon became a ritual. He himself was clad in white including his socks and footwear.

In all practicality, people do not usually stock up white attire, let alone have a matching outfit from head to toe. Many may not have budgeted for such an eventuality, and could not afford it. Some may simply not wish to be in white. Others who could secure the all-white outfit may not feel that pure just by wearing them, and could develop a guilty complex. A few others attended the service in colored clothes but felt out of place. These and many other reasons could deter people from going to church. As the Holy Spirit is not interested in hindrances to attending church, this opens the door for people to question the source of the revelation or the interpretation of it. If you have knowledge, you realize that it is the water spirit that would seek to regularize an all-white outfit for church services or so-called special occasions. As already mentioned, the "white garment" sects began that way; and we also know from 2 Corinthians 11:14 that satan masquerades as an angel of light or an angel in white appearance. We have to bear in mind that the outward appearance does not guarantee holiness or purity within, even if your outfit may reflect your "infit".

Please also note that this is not directed at the Salvation Army's white uniforms in tropical countries, which is simply for reasons of the weather, because the white color absorbs the least heat in the hot temperatures; their counterparts in cold weather countries wear dark or black uniforms, because the color black absorbs and retains the most heat or warmth for the cold temperatures.

Chapter 12

Culture: the shadow of things to come

Key Texts

- ✓ Colossians 2:16 & 17
- ✓ Isaiah 1:13–16 ; 18–20
- ✓ Genesis 10:5
- ✓ Revelation 5:9–10

Every culture and its demonstrations will manifest attributes of the Creator. In the attempt to imitate divine orders (the things given or things to come), culture (the shadow of things to come) gets in the way, so that human beings introduce, copy or produce imitations and counterfeit. The difference or bridge between the exact pattern God has shown you, and how you manifest it, is the culture. Culture is the tradition about food, drink, and clothes or the things that are worn to reflect whatever the occasion might be – whether a festival, new moon or sabbath, and the behaviors associated with such occasions in any society, which tend to perpetuate, and inherently become cultural traditions. We have already highlighted in our discussion in Chapter 11 on dreaming and dressing, that one can be very creative. Indirectly, culture can get in the way of Godly patterns, in addition to direct action of satan and satanic agents to pervert the divine. Hence we should be ourselves and not be pretentious, and also be careful not to let our culture dictate to the Holy Spirit. God created different peoples and cultures, and Colossians 2:16 & 17 therefore states: "So let no one judge you in food or in drink, or regarding a festival or a new moon or sabbaths, which are a shadow of things to come, but the substance is of Christ. Let no one cheat you of your reward, taking delight in false humility and worship of angels, intruding into those things which he has not seen, vainly puffed up by his fleshly mind."

Because culture is a grey area, and we are not to judge (unless pinpointed expressly by the Holy Spirit), some take advantage of this grey area, and covertly or overtly grieve the Holy Spirit with their culture. Yes, scripture says we should not be judged by "food, drink, festival, new moon or sabbaths", but just because we should be at liberty does not mean we should take liberties and do what God has instructed against. For example, there are "white garment" sects, the "celestial" or "cherubim and seraphim" sects, and religious groups of similar persuasions, who regularly use incense, while others partake in special moons and sabbaths. However scripture is clear from Isaiah 1:13–16 that incense is an abomination, and God hates new moons, sabbaths and the appointed feasts related to them. Therefore, God provided a solution in the immediate verses following (Isaiah 1:18–20), that "come now and let us reason together … though your sins are like scarlet, they shall be as white as snow." Let us simply obey

God instead of trying to appease Him through incense and festivities, or trying to appeal to Him with white attire.

After Noah survived the great deluge, the Old Testament describes his descendants as peoples by language, families and nations (Genesis 10:5), which means the linguistic, cultural, and racial distinctions of humanity do originate from the Creator. In the New Testament, this changes from "every tribe and tongue and people and nation" (Revelation 5:9) to the potential to be redeemed by the blood of the Lamb and translated into a new identity of kings and priests to God, to reign on the earth with the Lamb (Revelation 5:10). Across the globe, the existing differences in race, culture, style, and musical tastes, do influence or impact on the style of worship, worship-leading, and church musicality as a whole. However, we pray that all believers will have the total liberty in the redemption by the Lamb, to demonstrate and manifest our full potential in the Holy Spirit, solely as kings and priests, in the worship and praise of God, without any cultural inhibitions or interferences.

Chapter 13

Giving as an act of Worship

Key Texts

- ✓ John 3:16
- ✓ John 1:12–13
- ✓ John 4:24
- ✓ Matthew 10:8
- ✓ Jeremiah 33:11
- ✓ Psalm 107:22 ; 116:17
- ✓ Hebrews 13:15
- ✓ Psalm 54:6
- ✓ Proverbs 11:24

Sometimes your love for God can manifest itself in offering or giving Him something as an act of worship. The Bible states that "for God so loved the world that He gave ..." (John 3:16). Hence giving is an act of love. Also, love is a relationship, which means that if you don't have a relationship with God, if you're not born-again or saved (John 1:12–13), or if you are not able to engage Him spirit-to-Spirit (John 4:24), then your giving is not an act of worship, but an act of praise, thanksgiving or sacrifice, which every human being (both saved and unsaved) is able to perform. In other words, if you are not a Christian, your giving is an act of charity and not an act of worship. If you are a Christian, then your giving is both a charitable act and an act of worship. Please note that giving as an act of worship is perverse when people visit evil altars or shrines to offer sacrifices as an act of worship to idols. Please also note that every deity demands a sacrifice, but God expects us to give freely or out of our freewill, just as we have received freely from Him (Matthew 10:8). The Bible mentions the sacrifice of praise (Jeremiah 33:11), and the sacrifices of thanksgiving in Psalms 107:22 and 116:17. As the sacrifice of thanksgiving is a freewill act of praise, Psalm 107:22 says it must be done with rejoicing. Hebrews 13:15 also says our sacrifice of praise is the fruit of our lips in giving thanks unto God. Hence Psalm 54:6 also states: "I will freely sacrifice to You, I will praise Your name, O Lord, for it is good." This also means, that giving in response to forms of coercion, extortion, intimidation, and manipulation is not an act of worship. Something about the manipulation, and the reluctance in the giving attitude under such manipulative circumstances, are a far cry from freewill offerings to God and to charity.

Chapter 14

God's plan of restoration to Worship

Key Texts

- ✓ John 4:24
- ✓ John 24:6
- ✓ John 1:12–13
- ✓ Mark 14:36
- ✓ Romans 8:15
- ✓ Galatians 4:6
- ✓ John 3:16
- ✓ John 1:1 ; John 1:14 ; John 3:16 ;
- ✓ Matthew 27 & 28
- ✓ 2 Timothy 2:5
- ✓ Romans 10:1–13
- ✓ Acts 4:12
- ✓ Hebrews 12:2

I reserved this chapter for last because I need to address all of humanity, including Christians, non-Christians, and whether or not you are interested in praise and worship. There is one thing that only human beings can do – and that is to worship God. There is also one thing which even God cannot do – and that is to worship Himself. Hence we as humans beings have been created by God to worship Him, because God (being a deity) is to be worshiped, and He has chosen us human beings to worship Him. This is an enormous privilege. The animals, trees, clouds, sun, moon and stars cannot worship God, they can only praise. Do you now see how special we are as human beings? Can you now understand what God (who cannot worship Himself) expects from us human beings?

I am aware that many people dislike the theology or biblical position that only those who are born-again can worship God. But that is the simple truth. Please note that this is not some matter which we have an option to do what we like: God says you must be born-again, and that is the bottom line. The scripture in John 4:24 says that "God is a Spirit, and those who worship Him must worship in spirit and truth." This is one particular scripture that every version of the Bible has it as a must. Also, God says in John 14:6 that "I am the way, the truth, and the life, no one comes to the Father except through me," and we cannot argue with this. So there is no argument about the theological position that only those who are born-again can worship God. Every human being is made up of spirit, soul, and body. Your body is flesh, and your mind is in the flesh. It is only your spirit that can relate to God spirit-to-Spirit, and without that, you cannot truly worship. So if God is using scripture to explain Himself to us, He is only trying to help us to understand Him. If you are a non-Christian, your unregenerate spirit (that is not born-again or born of God – John 1:13) would not qualify to worship God, or would not be able to worship God because you cannot relate to Him as Abba Father - you are not a child of God (John 1:12–13), and your spirit cannot cry to Him as Abba Father (Mark 14:36 / Romans 8:15 / Galatians 4:6). So I would encourage you to receive Jesus Christ into your life as your personal savior, and become born-again (John 1:12–13).

I do appreciate why you are baffled or annoyed that you have been created by God, yet if you are not born-again, someone keeps referring to you as not being a child of God. In the beginning, our ancestors Adam and Eve who lived in the Garden of Eden had direct access to God, until they sinned and lost their right standing with Him (Genesis 3:1–13). Because God loves humanity that much (John 3:16), He devised a plan to restore that right-standing between Himself and humanity. So God sent His only son Jesus Christ who lived with Him (John 1:1) to come down to earth as a human being and live with humanity (John 1:14). In this plan of restoration, Jesus Christ was crucified on the earth to take away the sins of humanity by the shedding of His blood on the cross, and resurrected on the third day (Matthew 27 & 28); and became the mediator between humanity and God (2 Timothy 2:5). When Jesus lived on the earth, He said "I am the way, the truth, and the life, no one comes to the Father except through me" (John 14:6). This means you must be restored through Jesus for that right-standing.

If you desire to have direct access to God as Adam and Eve did, you must receive Jesus as your mediator, "for there is one

God and one mediator between God and men, the man Christ Jesus" (2 Timothy 2:5). Once you receive Jesus, He gives you power to become a child of God (John 1:12–13) and then you are restored to God or saved, and then you can worship God in spirit and in truth. If you are reading this book, and you are wondering how this process takes place, or how you can be saved, or where to receive Jesus, it is a very simple process. But you must be prepared to believe and accept that Jesus is God's plan of restoration or salvation for your life. Once you have accepted this fact, the rest is easy. Romans 10:9–10 says that "if you confess with your mouth the Lord Jesus and believe in your heart that God has raised Him from the dead, you will be saved. For with the heart one believes unto righteousness, and with the mouth confession is made unto salvation." Romans 10:13 also says that "whoever calls on the name of the LORD shall be saved." But note one thing, that "there is no other name under heaven given among men by which we must be saved" (Acts 4:12). So you have no other option than to give your life to Jesus Christ, the author and the finisher of your faith (Hebrews 12:2).

God bless you.

Songs Composed by Michael Amoah

We Hail You Lord

Chorus

Halleluiah, You are Lord
You're the King of Kings
And Lord of Lords
We magnify your name
All the earth shall worship you
And sing unto your name
You are the mighty one
You are Lord

First Verse

Lord We hail you
We lift your name above all names
We say there's none like unto You
Holy is your name
At the mention of your name, Lord
Every knee shall bow
And every tongue shall confess
That you are Lord

Chorus

Halleluiah, You are Lord
You're the King of Kings
And Lord of Lords
We magnify your name

All the earth shall worship you
And sing unto your name
You are the mighty one
You are Lord

Second Verse

In the valley of the shadow of death
We shall fear no evil
Thy rod and thy staff
They comfort us
And we know You shall set our table
In the presence of our enemies
We're sure of your protection
You are Lord.

Chorus

HE IS OUR REDEMPTION

He Is Our Redemption

Celebrate the King of Kings
Halleluiah, He is our King

Wave your hands unto the King
Worship Jesus King of the Universe

He is our redemption
Song of Songs
Our Salvation
Christ is King

Celebration
Christ is Lord
Halleluiah
Christ is King

Halleluiah
Christ is King
King of the Universe
King of Kings

Come Kingdom Come
Will be done
In earth and Heaven
He's ready to save

He is our Redeemer
Son of God
He can save now
Jesus Christ

Halleluiah
King of Kings
Halleluiah
Christ is Alive!

Copyright © Michael Amoah March 1995
First released in London KT 1995 at Students Ministries
Saturday Night in the midst of the London revival

We Rejoice

First Verse
He has kindled our hearts
Made us rich in His Glory
Supplies of riches in glory
He's given us

Grace abundant He's given, yeah
A mighty crop He will harvest, yeah
We are ready to reap
And we rejoice

Make your labor available
Get your sickles ready
The land is rich for the harvest
We rejoice

Make your labor available
Get your sickles ready
The land is rich for the harvest
We rejoice

Chorus

Let us give thanks to God Almighty
Let us give thanks to God our King
He's enriched our souls
And we rejoice

Let us give thanks to God Almighty
Let us give thanks to God our King
He has filled our lives
And we rejoice

Second Verse

A shoal of fish in the sea, yeah
Big and small fish alike, yeah
String nets spread awide
In the river of life

Are you ready to swim, yeah
Are you ready to dive and deep
We reach out in deep seas
And draw them in

Is your vessel available
To sail in the tide of the sea of love
You can swim in the deep
If you will drink

Is your vessel available
To sail in the tide of the sea of love
You can swim in the deep
If you will drink

Chorus

Let us give thanks to God Almighty
Let us give thanks to God our King
He's enriched our souls
And we rejoice

Let us give thanks to God Almighty
Let us give thanks to God our King
He has filled our lives
And we rejoice

Third Verse

Are you ready to dance and sing
Are you ready to praise the Lord
Shouts of joy and dancing
We rejoice

Hail the King of Glory, yeah
Dance to the tune of His triumph, yeah
Here He comes with healing
In His wings

All ye people clap your hands
Shout with a voice of triumph
He's the Almighty King
And we rejoice

All ye people clap your hands
Shout with a voice of triumph
He's the Almighty King
And we rejoice

Chorus

Let us give thanks to God Almighty
Let us give thanks to God our King
He's enriched our souls
And we rejoice

Let us give thanks to God Almighty
Let us give thanks to God our King
He has filled our lives
And we rejoice

Love is the Spirit

Verse

Love is the Spirit that enables me
Kind is the Saviour who gave me the Spirit
Out of the abundance of the heart
The mouths of the saints will glorify His name

Chorus

So Jesus
I praise You
I thank you
I love You
I will worship You
I'll adore You

Copyright © 1988 Michael Amoah